Great Works

Instructional Guides for Literature

MY FATHER'S DRAGON

A guide for the book by Ruth Stiles Gannett
Great Works Author: Ashley Scott

SHELL EDUCATION

Publishing Credits

Robin Erickson, *Production Director;* Lee Aucoin, *Creative Director;*
Timothy J. Bradley, *Illustration Manager;* Emily R. Smith, M.A.Ed., *Editorial
Director;* Amber Goff, *Editorial Assistant;* Don Tran, *Production Supervisor;*
Corinne Burton, M.A.Ed., *Publisher*

Image Credits

Timothy J. Bradley (cover, pages 11–12, pages 61–63)

Standards

© 2007 Teachers of English to Speakers of Other Languages, Inc. (TESOL)
© 2007 Board of Regents of the University of Wisconsin System. World-Class Instructional Design and Assessment (WIDA)
© Copyright 2010. National Governors Association Center for Best Practices and Council of Chief State School Officers.
All rights reserved.

Shell Education

5301 Oceanus Drive
Huntington Beach, CA 92649-1030
http://www.shelleducation.com

ISBN 978-1-4258-8968-5

© 2014 Shell Educational Publishing, Inc.

Table of Contents

How to Use This Literature Guide

Today's standards demand rigor and relevance in the reading of complex texts. The units in this series guide teachers in a rich and deep exploration of worthwhile works of literature for classroom study. The most rigorous instruction can also be interesting and engaging!

Many current strategies for effective literacy instruction have been incorporated into these instructional guides for literature. Throughout the units, text-dependent questions are used to determine comprehension of the book as well as student interpretation of the vocabulary words. The books chosen for the series are complex and are exemplars of carefully crafted works of literature. Close reading is used throughout the units to guide students toward revisiting the text and using textual evidence to respond to prompts orally and in writing. Students must analyze the story elements in multiple assignments for each section of the book. All of these strategies work together to rigorously guide students through their study of literature.

The next few pages describe how to use this guide for a purposeful and meaningful literature study. Each section of this guide is set up in the same way to make it easier for you to implement the instruction in your classroom.

Theme Thoughts

The great works of literature used throughout this series have important themes that have been relevant to people for many years. Many of the themes will be discussed during the various sections of this instructional guide. However, it would also benefit students to have independent time to think about the key themes of the book.

Before students begin reading, have them complete the *Pre-Reading Theme Thoughts* (page 13). This graphic organizer will allow students to think about the themes outside the context of the story. They'll have the opportunity to evaluate statements based on important themes and defend their opinions. Be sure to keep students' papers for comparison to the *Post-Reading Theme Thoughts* (page 59). This graphic organizer is similar to the pre-reading activity. However, this time, students will be answering the questions from the point of view of one of the characters in the book. They have to think about how the character would feel about each statement and defend their thoughts. To conclude the activity, have students compare what they thought about the themes before they read the book to what the characters discovered during the story.

How to Use This Literature Guide (cont.)

Vocabulary

Each teacher reference vocabulary overview page has definitions and sentences about how key vocabulary words are used in the section. These words should be introduced and discussed with students. Students will use these words in different activities throughout the book.

On some of the vocabulary student pages, students are asked to answer text-related questions about vocabulary words from the sections. The following question stems will help you create your own vocabulary questions if you'd like to extend the discussion.

- How does this word describe _____'s character?
- How does this word connect to the problem in this story?
- How does this word help you understand the setting?
- Tell me how this word connects to the main idea of this story.
- What visual pictures does this word bring to your mind?
- Why do you think the author used this word?

At times, you may find that more work with the words will help students understand their meanings and importance. These quick vocabulary activities are a good way to further study the words.

- Students can play vocabulary concentration. Make one set of cards that has the words on them and another set with the definitions. Then, have students lay them out on the table and play concentration. The goal of the game is to match vocabulary words with their definitions. For early readers or English language learners, the two sets of cards could be the words and pictures of the words.

- Students can create word journal entries about the words. Students choose words they think are important and then describe why they think each word is important within the book. Early readers or English language learners could instead draw pictures about the words in a journal.

- Students can create puppets and use them to act out the vocabulary words from the stories. Students may also enjoy telling their own character-driven stories using vocabulary words from the original stories.

How to Use This Literature Guide (cont.)

Analyzing the Literature

After you have read each section with students, hold a small-group or whole-class discussion. Provided on the teacher reference page for each section are leveled questions. The questions are written at two levels of complexity to allow you to decide which questions best meet the needs of your students. The Level 1 questions are typically less abstract than the Level 2 questions. These questions are focused on the various story elements, such as character, setting, and plot. Be sure to add further questions as your students discuss what they've read. For each question, a few key points are provided for your reference as you discuss the book with students.

Reader Response

In today's classrooms, there are often great readers who are below average writers. So much time and energy is spent in classrooms getting students to read on grade level that little time is left to focus on writing skills. To help teachers include more writing in their daily literacy instruction, each section of this guide has a literature-based reader response prompt. Each of the three genres of writing is used in the reader responses within this guide: narrative, informative/explanatory, and opinion. Before students write, you may want to allow them time to draw pictures related to the topic. Book-themed writing paper is provided on pages 69–70 if your students need more space to write.

Guided Close Reading

Within each section of this guide, it is suggested that you closely reread a portion of the text with your students. Page numbers are given, but since some versions of the books may have different page numbers, the sections to be reread are described by location as well. After rereading the section, there are a few text-dependent questions to be answered by students. Working space has been provided to help students prepare for the group discussion. They should record their thoughts and ideas on the activity page and refer to it during your discussion. Rather than just taking notes, you may want to require students to write complete responses to the questions before discussing them with you.

Encourage students to read one question at a time and then go back to the text and discover the answer. Work with students to ensure that they use the text to determine their answers rather than making unsupported inferences. Suggested answers are provided in the answer key.

How to Use This Literature Guide (cont.)

Guided Close Reading (cont.)

The generic open-ended stems below can be used to write your own text-dependent questions if you would like to give students more practice.

- What words in the story support . . . ?
- What text helps you understand . . . ?
- Use the book to tell why _____ happens.
- Based on the events in the story, . . . ?
- Show me the part in the text that supports . . . .
- Use the text to tell why . . . .

Making Connections

The activities in this section help students make cross-curricular connections to mathematics, science, social studies, fine arts, or other curricular areas. These activities require higher-order thinking skills from students but also allow for creative thinking.

Language Learning

A special section has been set aside to connect the literature to language conventions. Through these activities, students will have opportunities to practice the conventions of standard English grammar, usage, capitalization, and punctuation.

Story Elements

It is important to spend time discussing what the common story elements are in literature. Understanding the characters, setting, plot, and theme can increase students' comprehension and appreciation of the story. If teachers begin discussing these elements in early childhood, students will more likely internalize the concepts and look for the elements in their independent reading. Another very important reason for focusing on the story elements is that students will be better writers if they think about how the stories they read are constructed.

In the story elements activities, students are asked to create work related to the characters, setting, or plot. Consider having students complete only one of these activities. If you give students a choice on this assignment, each student can decide to complete the activity that most appeals to him or her. Different intelligences are used so that the activities are diverse and interesting to all students.

How to Use This Literature Guide (cont.)

Culminating Activity

At the end of this instructional guide is a creative culminating activity that allows students the opportunity to share what they've learned from reading the book. This activity is open ended so that students can push themselves to create their own great works within your language arts classroom.

Comprehension Assessment

The questions in this section require students to think about the book they've read as well as the words that were used in the book. Some questions are tied to quotations from the book to engage students and require them to think about the text as they answer the questions.

Response to Literature

Finally, students are asked to respond to the literature by drawing pictures and writing about the characters and stories. A suggested rubric is provided for teacher reference.

Correlation to the Standards

Shell Education is committed to producing educational materials that are research and standards based. As part of this effort, we have correlated all of our products to the academic standards of all 50 states, the District of Columbia, the Department of Defense Dependents Schools, and all Canadian provinces.

Purpose and Intent of Standards

Standards are designed to focus instruction and guide adoption of curricula. Standards are statements that describe the criteria necessary for students to meet specific academic goals. They define the knowledge, skills, and content students should acquire at each level. Standards are also used to develop standardized tests to evaluate students' academic progress. Teachers are required to demonstrate how their lessons meet standards. Standards are used in the development of all of our products, so educators can be assured they meet high academic standards.

How To Find Standards Correlations

To print a customized correlation report of this product for your state, visit our website at http://www.shelleducation.com and follow the online directions. If you require assistance in printing correlation reports, please contact our Customer Service Department at 1-877-777-3450.

Correlation to the Standards (cont.)

Standards Correlation Chart

The lessons in this book were written to support the Common Core College and Career Readiness Anchor Standards. The following chart indicates which lessons address the anchor standards.

Common Core College and Career Readiness Anchor Standard	Section
CCSS.ELA-Literacy.CCRA.R.1—Read closely to determine what the text says explicitly and to make logical inferences from it; cite specific textual evidence when writing or speaking to support conclusions drawn from the text.	Analyzing the Literature Sections 1–5; Guided Close Reading Sections 1–5
CCSS.ELA-Literacy.CCRA.R.2—Determine central ideas or themes of a text and analyze their development; summarize the key supporting details and ideas.	Analyzing the Literature Sections 1–5; Guided Close Reading Sections 1–5; Post-Reading Theme Thoughts
CCSS.ELA-Literacy.CCRA.R.3—Analyze how and why individuals, events, or ideas develop and interact over the course of a text.	Analyzing the Literature Sections 1–5; Guided Close Reading Sections 1–5; Story Elements Sections 1–4; Post-Reading Theme Thoughts
CCSS.ELA-Literacy.CCRA.R.4—Interpret words and phrases as they are used in a text, including determining technical, connotative, and figurative meanings, and analyze how specific word choices shape meaning or tone.	Vocabulary Sections 1–5, Making Connections Section 5
CCSS.ELA-Literacy.CCRA.R.5—Analyze the structure of texts, including how specific sentences, paragraphs, and larger portions of the text (e.g., a section, chapter, scene, or stanza) relate to each other and the whole.	Post-Reading Response to Literature
CCSS.ELA-Literacy.CCRA.R.10—Read and comprehend complex literary and informational texts independently and proficiently.	Entire Unit
CCSS.ELA-Literacy.CCRA.W.1—Write arguments to support claims in an analysis of substantive topics or texts using valid reasoning and relevant and sufficient evidence.	Reader Response Section 3; Story Elements Section 4
CCSS.ELA-Literacy.CCRA.W.2—Write informative/explanatory texts to examine and convey complex ideas and information clearly and accurately through the effective selection, organization, and analysis of content.	Reader Response Sections 1, 5

Correlation to the Standards (cont.)

Standards Correlation Chart (cont.)

Common Core College and Career Readiness Anchor Standard	Section
CCSS.ELA-Literacy.CCRA.W.3—Write narratives to develop real or imagined experiences or events using effective technique, well-chosen details and well-structured event sequences.	Reader Response Sections 1, 4; Story Elements Sections 3; Language Learning Section 2; Making Connections Sections 4–5
CCSS.ELA-Literacy.CCRA.W.4—Produce clear and coherent writing in which the development, organization, and style are appropriate to task, purpose, and audience.	Making Connections Section 1; Story Elements Sections 2–5; Reader Response Sections 1–5
CCSS.ELA-Literacy.CCRA.L.1—Demonstrate command of the conventions of standard English grammar and usage when writing or speaking.	Reader Response Sections 1–5; Language Learning Sections 1–2, 4–5
CCSS.ELA-Literacy.CCRA.L.2—Demonstrate command of the conventions of standard English capitalization, punctuation, and spelling when writing.	Reader Response Sections 1–5; Language Learning Sections 3
CCSS.ELA-Literacy.CCRA.L.4—Determine or clarify the meaning of unknown and multiple-meaning words and phrases by using context clues, analyzing meaningful word parts, and consulting general and specialized reference materials, as appropriate.	Vocabulary Sections 1–5
CCSS.ELA-Literacy.CCRA.L.5—Demonstrate understanding of figurative language, word relationships, and nuances in word meanings.	Language Learning Section 4
CCSS.ELA-Literacy.CCRA.L.6—Acquire and use accurately a range of general academic and domain-specific words and phrases sufficient for reading, writing, speaking, and listening at the college and career readiness level; demonstrate independence in gathering vocabulary knowledge when encountering an unknown term important to comprehension or expression.	Vocabulary Sections 1–5

TESOL and WIDA Standards

The lessons in this book promote English language development for English language learners. The following TESOL and WIDA English Language Development Standards are addressed through the activities in this book:

- **Standard 1:** English language learners communicate for social and instructional purposes within the school setting.
- **Standard 2:** English language learners communicate information, ideas and concepts necessary for academic success in the content area of language arts.

About the Author—Ruth Stiles Gannett

Ruth Stiles Gannett was born on August 12, 1923, in New York City. As a child, Gannett spent most of her summers in Connecticut where she entertained herself writing and creating. She went to the City and Country School in Greenwich Village, where she benefited from being encouraged to write for fun during the day.

Later in her childhood, Gannett left New York City to attend a Quaker boarding school in Newton, Pennsylvania. Eventually, she attended Vassar College where she studied chemistry. Upon graduation, Gannett worked in the medical research field at both Boston College Hospital and the Massachusetts Institute of Technology. She married artist and calligrapher Peter Kahn. They had seven daughters.

In 1946, while between jobs, Gannett wrote *My Father's Dragon* mostly as a way to pass time and with no intention of publishing it. With the encouragement of her daughters and after a chance encounter with an editor at Random House, *My Father's Dragon* was accepted for publication. *My Father's Dragon* became a family effort when Gannett's stepmother illustrated the novel and her husband chose the font type. The book became an immediate success and even won a Newbery Honor. It took first place in book festivals in 1948 and 1949 and has since been translated into 10 languages. Gannett went on to write two sequels to *My Father's Dragon—Elmer and the Dragon* and *The Dragons of Blueland*. All three of these beloved children's books have been in continuous print since their inception. Gannett also wrote two more books, *Katie and the Sad Noise* and *The Wonderful House-Boat-Train*.

Gannett credits her happy childhood as inspiration for her story ideas. She now has many grandchildren and is retired and living in New York State, where she is able to practice her beloved hobbies of spinning and dyeing.

Possible Texts for Text Comparisons

There are two other books in this Ruth Stiles Gannett series: *Elmer and the Dragon* and *The Dragons of Blueland*. *Katie and the Sad Noise* and *The Wonderful House-Boat-Train* may also be used for enriching text comparisons by the same author.

Cross-Curricular Connection

This book can be used in a science unit on the study of animal habitats or in a social studies unit on map skills.

Book Summary of *My Father's Dragon*

My Father's Dragon is the story of a little boy named Elmer Elevator who goes on an exciting journey to rescue a dragon from an island filled with lazy but ferocious animals. The story begins with Elmer befriending a stray cat. Elmer's mother yells at him to get rid of the cat. Upset and sad, Elmer takes a walk with the cat. While walking, they begin talking and Elmer reveals that he has always dreamed of flying. The cat tells Elmer about a baby dragon who is held captive on a mysterious island. The baby dragon fell from a cloud to Wild Island, where a group of animals tied him to a stake. They force him to serve as a ferry, flying all the lazy animals across a wide river. The cat tells Elmer that if he frees the dragon, the dragon will be so grateful to Elmer for rescuing him that he will offer to fly Elmer anywhere he wants to go.

Elmer and the cat begin to plot his upcoming journey and the supplies needed for his adventure. Elmer must make the trip alone as the cat is too old to travel that far. Elmer hides on board a ship that takes him to the Island of Tangerina. Once he arrives, Elmer travels to Wild Island, which is connected to Tangerina by a rock bridge. Following the cat's advice, Elmer is careful not to travel during daylight.

Elmer consistently finds himself stumbling upon charismatic jungle animals. Each animal is intent on causing harm to Elmer, but due to his ingenuity, resourcefulness, and bravery Elmer is able to play upon each animal's character flaw and devise a way to escape. Elmer is always one step ahead of the wild pack of beasts that pursues him. The reader is continuously amazed and amused by Elmer's quick wit and use of his unique bag of supplies. Eventually, Elmer is able to reach the dragon.

Possible Texts for Text Sets

- Calhoun, Mary. *Cross-Country Cat.* Mulberry Books, 1986.

- Prelutsky, Jack. *The Dragons Are Singing Tonight.* Greenwillow Books, 1998.

- Seabrooke, Brenda. *The Dragon That Ate Summer.* Putnam Juvenile, 1992.

- Thomson, Sarah L. *Dragon's Egg.* Greenwillow Books, 2010.

Name _____ Date _____

Pre-Reading Theme Thoughts

Directions: For each statement, draw a picture of a happy face or a sad face. Your face should show how you feel about the statement. Then, use words to say why you feel that way.

Statement	How Do You Feel? ☺ ☹	Explain Your Answer
Helping others is very important.		
Getting others to do your work is fair.		
If you are scared, then you are not being brave.		
It is better to solve problems with your brain than with violence.		

Vocabulary Overview

Key words and phrases from this section are provided below with definitions and sentences about how the words are used in the story. Introduce and discuss these important vocabulary words with students. If you think these words or other words in the story warrant more time devoted to them, there are suggestions in the introduction for other vocabulary activities (page 5).

Word	Definition	Sentence about Text
obliged (ch. 1)	grateful for something that was done	The cat feels **obliged** to Elmer because Elmer helps him.
cellar (ch. 1)	basement	The **cellar** where the cat drinks her milk is dark and chilly.
inhabited (ch. 1)	lived in, was a resident of	Wild animals **inhabit** the island.
weep (ch. 1)	to cry heavily	Thinking about the dragon makes the cat want to **weep**.
inconvenient (ch. 2)	not well timed; something that is difficult or annoying to do	It is **inconvenient** for the animals to walk around the river on the island.
stake (ch. 2)	a wooden stick sharpened on one end	The dragon is tied to a **stake** in the ground to keep him from flying away.
knapsack (ch. 2)	backpack	Elmer carries a **knapsack** of supplies to Wild Island.
docks (ch. 2)	places in a harbor where ships tie up	The ship is sitting at the **dock** when Elmer boards.
queer (ch. 2)	unusual; weird	The cat makes **queer** noises to distract the night watchman.
gangplank (ch. 2)	a temporary bridge used to get on and off a boat	Elmer runs over the **gangplank** to get on the ship.

Name _____ Date _____

Vocabulary Activity

Directions: Choose at least two words from the story. Draw a picture that shows what these words mean. Label your picture.

Words from the Story

obliged	cellar	inhabited	weep	inconvenient
stake	knapsack	docks	queer	gangplank

Directions: Answer this question.

1. The animals **inhabited** which island?

_____

Analyzing the Literature

Provided below are discussion questions you can use in small groups, with the whole class, or for written assignments. Each question is written at two levels so that you can choose the right question for each group of students. For each question, a few key points are provided for your reference as you discuss the book with students.

Story Element	Level 1	Level 2	Key Discussion Points
Setting	How do the animals cross the wide river that splits the island?	Describe the impact the river has on the animals.	The river is long and almost divides the island in half. The animals have to walk around the river to get to the other side of the island. They are too lazy to do this so they get the dragon to fly them across.
Plot	What problem does the dragon have that makes him so miserable?	Explain the multiple problems so far in this story.	The dragon is held captive on the island by the other animals. He is forced to fly the animals across the river so they do not have to walk around it. Elmer has a problem with wanting things but being too young for them. The cat has a problem in the beginning with being homeless and hungry.
Plot	Why do Elmer and the cat keep the trip a secret?	How would the story have been affected if Elmer's plans for a secret trip had been discovered?	Elmer's mom does not like him taking care of the alley cat. She would have been very upset had she found out Elmer is planning to rescue a dragon. Elmer would have had to stay home and the dragon would continue to be held captive.
Character	Why isn't Elmer sad to run away from home?	Provide evidence from the book to support why Elmer isn't sad to leave home.	Elmer's mother does not want to help the cat, and she becomes very angry with Elmer. He runs away to escape his own miserable life at home. Students may make the connection that Elmer identifies with the dragon, which is why he wants to help the dragon escape.

Name _____ Date _____

Reader Response

Think

Think about a time when you have taken care of an animal, a friend, or a family member.

Narrative Writing Prompt

Elmer takes care of the cat by giving her food and water. Tell about a time when you helped take care of an animal or someone in your life.

_____

_____

_____

_____

_____

_____

_____

_____

Name _____ Date _____

Guided Close Reading

Closely reread the paragraph near the end of chapter 2 that begins, "Everything had to be kept very secret . . . ." This paragraph lists the items Elmer packs in the knapsack.

Directions: Think about these questions. In the chart, write ideas or draw pictures as you think. Be ready to share your answers.

❶ Choose at least four items from the list. Based on the story, how do you think Elmer might use these items during his journey?

❷ In what ways does this list support the idea that Elmer is brave?

❸ Which items are things that you might pack for an adventure on a wild island?

Name _____ Date _____

Making Connections-A Bag Full of Tricks!

Directions: Elmer packs his knapsack full of supplies that he believes will be useful on the island. Below is a list of the items that Elmer packs. Use these items to write at least three math word problems. An example has been provided for your reference.

• 7 pieces of chewing gum	• 1 toothbrush	• 1 jackknife	• 1 compass
• 2 black rubber boots	• 25 sandwiches	• 1 toothpaste	• 6 apples
• a package of 17 rubber bands	• 7 hair ribbons	• 1 comb	• 1 hairbrush
• 6 magnifying glasses	• 1 empty grain bag	• 24 pink lollipops	• 2 sets of clean clothes

1. Elmer places the comb, hairbrush, and 7 hair ribbons into the empty grain bag. How many items does he have in the bag?

2. _____

_____

3. _____

_____

4. _____

_____

Name _____ Date _____

Language Learning–Adjectives

Directions: Both the animals and Elmer want the dragon. So, the dragon is an important character in the story. Fill the box with pictures and adjectives about the dragon. Be sure to include details both about the dragon's looks and personality. Use color to make your picture bright and bold.

Language Hints!

- Adjectives describe nouns.

- Common types of adjectives: colors, numbers, sounds, shapes, and weather

Name _____ Date _____

Story Elements-Character

Directions: The cat meets Elmer when she is homeless and very hungry. The cat has traveled a lot. Write a story describing an adventure that the cat may have had prior to meeting Elmer.

_____

_____

_____

_____

_____

_____

_____

_____

_____

_____

_____

_____

Name _____ Date _____

Story Elements—Setting

Directions: Look at the map of Wild Island on the page before chapter 2. Using this as a model, create a map of your own island. It should be similar to Wild Island in some ways. Your map should show plants, animals, and landforms.

Vocabulary Overview

Key words and phrases from this section are provided below with definitions and sentences about how the words are used in the story. Introduce and discuss these important vocabulary words with students. If you think these words or other words in the story warrant more time devoted to them, there are suggestions in the introduction for other vocabulary activities (page 5).

Word	Definition	Sentence about Text
cargo (ch. 3)	goods carried by a large ship	Elmer hides in the ship next to the cargo.
merchant (ch. 3)	a person who sells goods or services	The merchant doesn't realize that Elmer is hiding in one of his bags of grain.
punctual (ch. 3)	on time	The punctual merchant is never late for dinner.
rumbling (ch. 3)	a heavy, continuous sound	Elmer can hear the rumbling noise of the snoring whale from far away.
narrow (ch. 4)	opposite of wide; really thin and skinny	There is a narrow area of beach just before the jungle starts.
damp (ch. 4)	moist or lightly wet	The sand near the beach on the island is damp.
solemn (ch. 4)	serious	The wild animals are solemn when they think that someone has entered their island.
invasion (ch. 4)	coming to an area when unwanted	A mouse is the first to notice the invasion of the island by Elmer.
extraordinary (ch. 4)	highly unusual or remarkable	The mouse thinks Elmer is an extraordinary rock.
unreliable (ch. 4)	not worthy of trust	The other animals believe mice are unreliable and do not believe there is an invasion.

Name _____ Date _____

Vocabulary Activity

Directions: Draw lines to match the sentences.

Beginnings of the Sentences	Endings of the Sentences
Elmer goes on an adventure	so the merchant is a punctual man.
As Elmer gets closer to Wild Island,	discuss the possibility of an intruder on the island.
He is never late to an important meeting,	because of the extraordinary cat.
The mouse is considered to be unreliable,	the rumbling noise of the snoring whale gets louder.
Solemn and nervous, the animals	so the animals do not believe him.

Directions: Answer this question.

1. What is the **invasion** that the animals keep talking about?

_____

Analyzing the Literature

Provided below are discussion questions you can use in small groups, with the whole class, or for written assignments. Each question is written at two levels so you can choose the right question for each group of students. For each question, a few key points are provided for your reference as you discuss the book with students.

Story Element	Level 1	Level 2	Key Discussion Points
Setting	What important resource does Elmer find when he wakes up under a tree his first morning off the ship?	How do the tangerines play an important role in chapters three and four?	Elmer wakes up under a tangerine tree. He realizes he can pack some tangerines to use as food. However, Elmer leaves peels around and that alerts the animals that someone may be on the island.
Character	What important lesson does Elmer learn after hearing the boars talk?	How do you think Elmer will change his habits now that the animals suspect there is an intruder?	Elmer leaves behind tangerine peels as he walks to the river. Elmer now will pick up his tangerine peels and be mindful not to leave any other obvious clues behind.
Plot	Elmer overhears the boars talking about him. How do you think the other animals will react to Elmer?	Based upon what you know about the way the boars react to the idea of an intruder, how do you think other animals will treat Elmer?	The animals are very upset and concerned that there is someone new on their island. Any animals Elmer comes across will most likely not be kind to him.
Character	What do the other animals think of mice?	Why do you think the boars consider the mouse to be unreliable?	The other animals believe mice are unreliable. Students can infer that this mouse has been wrong or has lied in the past. Also, the way that the mouse messes up his words makes him seem like an incompetent, silly character.

Name _____ Date _____

Reader Response

Think

Think about a time when you were scared or nervous because of a new adventure in your life.

Informative/Explanatory Writing Prompt

Describe what you do when you are scared or nervous. What steps do you take to feel better?

_____

_____

_____

_____

_____

_____

_____

_____

_____

Name _____ Date _____

Guided Close Reading

Closely reread where the animals begin to notice the signs of an invasion in chapter 4. Continue until the end of the chapter.

Directions: Think about these questions. In the chart, write ideas or draw pictures as you think. Be ready to share your answers.

❶ Use the text to find the two scary things that happen to Elmer.

❷ What does one of the boars say to show that he thinks he is the smartest animal?

❸ Use the book to figure out why Elmer continues and does not return home at this point.

Name _____ Date _____

Making Connections—What's Your Business?

Directions: Imagine that you are a merchant just like the one in chapter 3. Your business offers a variety of goods and services. Sort each of the following items into either the goods or services column. Add your own ideas for one good and one service in the last row.

A **good** is when an object is made. When a business makes shoes, clothing, or a book, it is selling a good.

A **service** is when a business does something for a customer. Examples of services are mowing lawns, cutting hair, and cleaning teeth.

wheat	loading a ship	tangerines	delivering bags
cranberries	baking bread	growing corn	fishing

Goods	Services

Name _____ Date _____

Language Learning–Writing Friendly Letters

Directions: Imagine you are Elmer and have been hiding in the hold of the ship for six days and nights. Write a letter to a friend that describes your thoughts and feelings as you get closer to the island.

Language Hints!

- Use a comma after your greeting.

- Use a comma after your closing.

_____

_____

_____

_____

_____

_____

_____

_____

                                          _____

                                          _____

Name_____ Date_____

Story Elements-Setting

Directions: Think about chapters 3 and 4 to help you fill in the following Venn diagram. Compare Wild Island to the Island of Tangerina. Be sure to include at least three details from the story to show how they are similar and how each island is different.

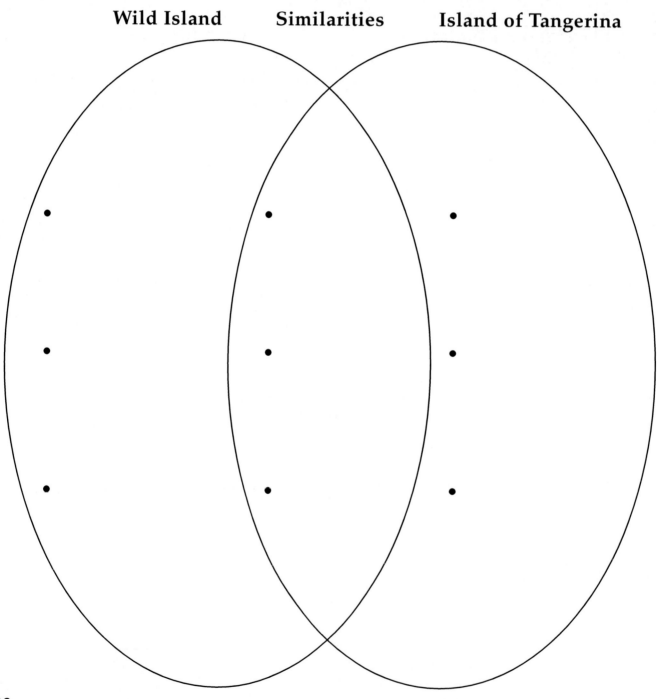

Wild Island   **Similarities**   **Island of Tangerina**

Name _____ Date _____

Story Elements-Plot

Directions: Elmer has many little adventures in these two chapters, like sleeping on a ship and stepping on a whale. Create a list of five events that happen to Elmer on his journey to find the river. Cut each event out in a strip. Then, give the events to a friend to glue in the order of how they happen in the book. Check your friend's work.

Vocabulary Overview

Key words and phrases from this section are provided below with definitions and sentences about how the words are used in the story. Introduce and discuss these important vocabulary words with students. If you think these words or other words in the story warrant more time devoted to them, there are suggestions in the introduction for other vocabulary activities (page 5).

Word	Definition	Sentence about Text
gloomy (ch. 5)	dark and dreary	The tall trees block out the sun causing it to be **gloomy** deep inside the jungle.
dense (ch. 5)	hard to walk through because it is thick	The jungle is **dense** with lots of trees.
bank (ch. 5)	the land along the edge of a river	It is easier for Elmer to walk along the **bank** of the river than to walk through the jungle.
clearing (ch. 5)	a small part of a forest or jungle that does not have any trees	Elmer comes across the tigers in a **clearing**.
contradict (ch. 5)	to say that something is not true	Elmer doesn't want to **contradict** a tiger when he is hungry.
scarce (ch. 5)	not enough of something	Gum is **scarce** on the island.
afoot (ch. 6)	happening	The boars know there is something **afoot** on the island.
waded (ch. 6)	walked through water that is not very deep	Elmer **wades** into the pond where the rhinoceros is sitting.
stooping (ch. 6)	bending down low	Elmer is **stooping** down in the water when the rhinoceros finds him.
dim (ch. 6)	not bright	The rhinoceros can't see his tusk very well in the **dim** light of the jungle.

Name _____ Date _____

Vocabulary Activity

Directions: Each of these sentences contains a word from the story. Cut apart these sentence strips. Put the sentences in order based on the events in the story.

The tigers are chewing gum, so the animals know there is an invasion **afoot**.

The **dim** jungle prevents Rhinoceros from seeing his tusk.

Elmer walks along the **bank** of the river.

Elmer **wades** in a small pool of water, not knowing what is in it.

Elmer is surrounded by seven tigers while in a **clearing**.

The jungle is too **dense** to walk through easily.

Analyzing the Literature

Provided below are discussion questions you can use in small groups, with the whole class, or for written assignments. Each question is written at two levels so you can choose the right question for each group of students. For each question, a few key points are provided for your reference as you discuss the book with students.

Story Element	Level 1	Level 2	Key Discussion Points
Setting	What obstacles does Elmer face during his walk along the river?	Describe Elmer's walk right up until he meets the tigers.	The riverbank is very muddy and swampy. It is hard to see through the dense jungle. Elmer struggles to walk and trips on tree roots.
Character	How would you describe the tigers and the rhinoceros?	What does the way Elmer tricks the tigers and Rhinoceros tell us about the animals?	The tigers are greedy because they want more chewing gum. Rhinoceros is vain and focused on making his tusk become white and beautiful. Both animals could be silly for falling for such simple tricks.
Character	What is the boars' reaction after seeing Rhinoceros?	What text tells us how the boars feel after seeing Rhinoceros?	The boars are angry and confused. They don't like that there is something disrupting all the other animals on Wild Island.
Plot	What two problems does Elmer encounter in these chapters?	Describe the two problems Elmer faces as well as his solutions.	The tigers want to eat Elmer. He tricks them by offering them chewing gum, which is a treat for them. Rhinoceros is upset over his ugly, yellow tusk. Elmer offers Rhinoceros a toothbrush and toothpaste to brighten his tusk.

Name _____ Date _____

Reader Response

Think

Think about what you know about tigers and rhinoceroses.

Opinion Writing Prompt

Would you rather meet a tiger or a rhinoceros? If you had to face one of these animals in the jungle, which one would you want to meet?

_____

_____

_____

_____

_____

_____

_____

_____

_____

#40100—Instructional Guide: My Father's Dragon

Name _____ Date _____

Guided Close Reading

Closely reread the beginning of chapter 5. This section describes Elmer's trek through the jungle. Stop when he hears "something laughing at him."

Directions: Think about these questions. In the chart, write ideas or draw pictures as you think. Be ready to share your answers.

❶ What words in the story describe what is hard about this part of Elmer's journey?

❷ Use words from the text to describe how Elmer navigates through the jungle.

❸ What details about this scene support the idea that Elmer is determined?

Name _____ Date _____

Making Connections-Time for Dinner!

The tigers want to eat Elmer, but not all animals eat meat. Read about the different names for animals based upon what they eat.

- Animals that mainly eat meat are called **carnivores**. They have very sharp teeth to help them bite through meat.

- Animals that eat only plants are called **herbivores**. They have flat teeth to help grind down the plants.

- Animals that eat both plants and animals are called **omnivores**. Omnivores have both sharp and flat teeth.

Directions: Draw a meal on each of the plates below to make each animal happy. Your meal should include at least three food items. Be sure to label each food item.

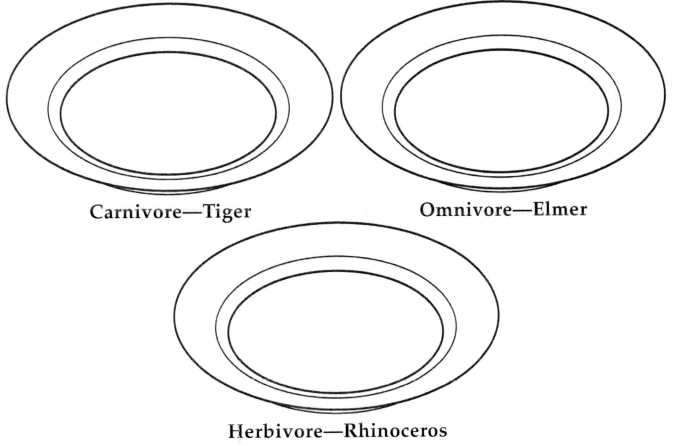

Carnivore—Tiger   Omnivore—Elmer

Herbivore—Rhinoceros

#40100—Instructional Guide: My Father's Dragon

Name _____ Date _____

Language Learning–Spelling

Directions: The words on this page are all found in this section of *My Father's Dragon*. Some of the words are spelled wrong on this page. Check the spelling and rewrite any misspelled words. Then, rewrite the words in alphabetical order.

Language Hints!

- Start alphabetizing with the first letter of each word.

- Compare words from left to right as you alphabetize.

Words from the Section	Alphabetize
jungle	_____
mud	_____
tegers	_____
trespasing	_____
hungry	_____
chuwing	_____
monkey	_____
dragoon	_____
private	_____
beatiful	_____

Name _____ Date _____

Story Elements-Plot

Directions: Fill in what happens next in the story.

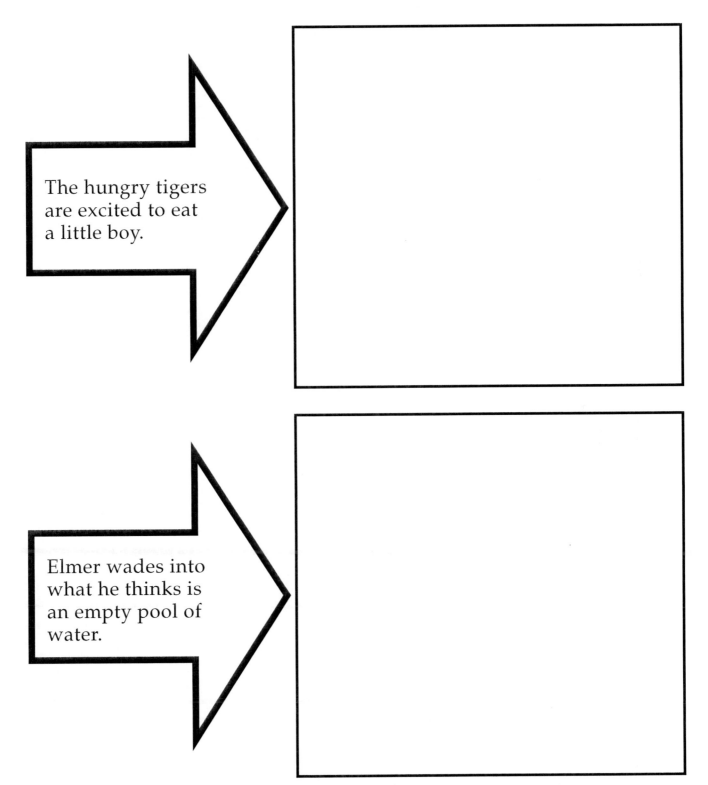

The hungry tigers are excited to eat a little boy.

Elmer wades into what he thinks is an empty pool of water.

#40100—Instructional Guide: My Father's Dragon

Name _____ Date _____

Story Elements-Characters

Directions: Pretend to be either a tiger or the rhinoceros. Rewrite a scene from the animal's perspective focusing on the events that happen when it comes across Elmer. Include how the animal feels when it first meets Elmer, why the animal does what Elmer says, and how the animal feels when it realizes it was tricked.

_____

_____

_____

_____

_____

_____

_____

_____

_____

_____

Vocabulary Overview

Key words and phrases from this section are provided below with definitions and sentences about how the words are used in the story. Introduce and discuss these important vocabulary words with students. If you think these words or other words in the story warrant more time devoted to them, there are suggestions in the introduction for other vocabulary activities (page 5).

Word	Definition	Sentence About Text
crept (ch. 7)	moved slowly and silently	Elmer **crept** up quietly to take a look at the lion.
prancing (ch. 7)	moving in an exaggerated, proud way	The lion comes **prancing** towards Elmer.
dreadful (ch. 7)	extremely bad	The lion's mane is a **dreadful** mess.
tidy (ch. 7)	clean and neat	The lion's mother likes her son's mane **tidy**.
forelock (ch. 7)	the part of a mane that grows in front of the ears	Elmer braids the lion's **forelock** first as an example.
grooming (ch. 7)	trying to make one's physical appearance look nice and neat	The lion is **grooming** his mane to make his mother happy.
dignified (ch. 8)	very proper and worthy of respect	The lioness walks in a **dignified** way with her nose in the air.
miraculous (ch. 8)	like a miracle	The monkeys think the magnifying glasses are **miraculous**.
frantically (ch. 8)	doing something very fast and maybe not with care	The monkeys **frantically** pick the fleas off the gorilla.
mangroves (ch. 8)	tropical trees	More monkeys come out of the **mangroves** to help clean off Gorilla.

Name _____ Date _____

Vocabulary Activity

Directions: Complete each sentence below with one of the vocabulary words listed here.

Words from the Story

crept	prancing	dreadful	tidy	forelock
grooming	dignified	miraculous	frantically	mangroves

1. Lion thinks his snarled, messy mane is _____.

2. Elmer quietly watches the _____ lioness walk by.

3. The monkeys think the magnifying glasses are

   _____.

4. The monkeys _____ try to get all the fleas off Gorilla.

Directions: Answer this question.

5. Why does Lion like to keep his mane **tidy**?

   _____

   _____

   _____

Analyzing the Literature

Provided below are discussion questions you can use in small groups, with the whole class, or for written assignments. Each question is written at two levels so that you can choose the right question for each group of students. For each question, a few key points are provided for your reference as you discuss the book with students.

Story Element	Level 1	Level 2	Key Discussion Points
Character	What will Lion lose if his mother does not like his mane?	What motive does Lion have to keep a tidy mane?	Lion's mother always wants him to have a tidy mane. If she does not approve of his mane, she may not give him his allowance. This makes Lion want to please his mother.
Setting	How does Elmer feel about how close he is to finding the dragon in chapter 8?	What words from the text describe how Elmer is feeling in chapter 8?	Elmer sees a sign pointing in the direction for "Dragon Ferry," and he sees Lion's mother. This makes him think that he is close to the dragon, but he soon realizes that he must be on the wrong side of the river.
Plot	What problem does Gorilla face?	What words in chapter 8 explain how Gorilla is feeling?	All the fleas on Gorilla frustrate him. He can feel them, but they are too small to see. He cannot get his work done with all the fleas bothering him.
Character	How do the supplies in Elmer's bag help him trick each animal?	Explain the pattern you notice in how Elmer solves every problem he faces with the animals.	Each animal has some reason why he is not happy. Elmer uses the supplies in his knapsack to make the animal feel better. The animal then becomes so busy that Elmer is able to escape.

Name _____ Date _____

Reader Response

Think

Think about the types of things you do to make people proud of you.

Narrative Writing Prompt

Lion is very nervous about making his mother happy. Tell about a time when you worked hard to make someone proud of you.

_____

_____

_____

_____

_____

_____

_____

_____

_____

#40100—Instructional Guide: My Father's Dragon   © Shell Education

Name _____ Date _____

Guided Close Reading

Closely reread the paragraph toward the beginning of chapter 8 that describes the crossroads Elmer finds. Begin with, "Before long my father came to a crossroads . . . ." Stop with, "He must have gone back to the other side."

Directions: Think about these questions. In the chart, write ideas or draw pictures as you think. Be ready to share your answers.

❶ Use the picture to determine which direction Elmer should take to find the dragon.

❷ What text evidence describes why Lion's mother does not notice Elmer?

❸ Based on the events in the story so far, describe a possible adventure Elmer might have if he chooses the wrong direction.

#40100—Instructional Guide: My Father's Dragon

Name _____ Date _____

Making Connections–Biomes of the World

Directions: This story takes place in the jungle. Choose another biome for the story to take place in. For example, you could choose the arctic, the ocean, or the desert. Then, write about an adventure Elmer could have with an animal from that new setting.

_____

_____

_____

_____

_____

_____

_____

_____

_____

_____

_____

_____

Name _____ Date _____

Language Learning–Alliteration

Directions: Gorilla hates having fleas on him. He asks for help from six monkeys: Rosie, Rhoda, Rachel, Ruthie, Ruby, and Roberta. Each name begins with an *R*. Good writers sometimes use alliteration to help make their writing more interesting. Try writing your own alliterative sentences about these characters.

Language Hints!

- Alliteration is when words start with the same letter.

- Small or unimportant words can start with other letters.

Example: Bossy Boar barks orders to beware of a bumbling burglar on the island.

Elmer _____

_____

Tigers _____

_____

Lion _____

_____

Gorilla _____

_____

Dragon _____

_____

Name _____ Date _____

Story Elements-Plot

Directions: The events in a story are part of the story's plot. Fill in the missing events from this story.

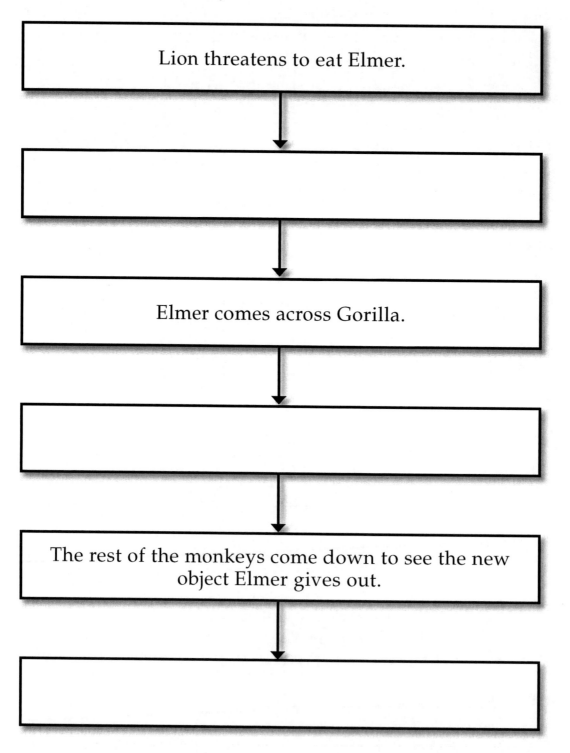

Lion threatens to eat Elmer.

Elmer comes across Gorilla.

The rest of the monkeys come down to see the new object Elmer gives out.

Name _____ Date _____

Story Elements-Character

Directions: Draw a picture showing how you think Lion's mother will react when she sees Lion's braided mane. Write a caption under your picture.

_____

_____

Vocabulary Overview

Key words and phrases from this section are provided below with definitions and sentences about how the words are used in the story. Introduce and discuss these important vocabulary words with students. If you think these words or other words in the story warrant more time devoted to them, there are suggestions in the introduction for other vocabulary activities (page 5).

Word	Definition	Sentence about Text
crank (ch. 9)	a machine used to help raise or lower a heavy load	A **crank** is attached to the dragon to make sure he doesn't escape.
summon (ch. 9)	to get someone's attention	A sign says to pull the crank to **summon** the dragon.
disorderly conduct (ch. 9)	bad behavior	Any **disorderly conduct** should be reported to Gorilla.
pale (ch. 9)	light in color	The **pale** moon gives off enough light for Elmer to see the animals coming.
fastened (ch. 9)	joined two objects together	Elmer **fastens** the lollipops to the alligators' tails.
seething (ch. 10)	extremely mad but holding it in	The animals are **seething** mad at the possibility of the dragon escaping.
countless (ch. 10)	so many that it is too hard or impossible to count	**Countless** monkeys chase after Elmer.
irate (ch. 10)	even more mad than furious	The boars are **irate** at Elmer.
spare (ch. 10)	having an extra of something	Elmer doesn't have a moment to **spare** when trying to release the dragon.
bellowing (ch. 10)	using a very loud voice	The animals are **bellowing** at Elmer and the dragon while they escape.

Name _____ Date _____

Vocabulary Activity

Directions: Practice your vocabulary and writing skills. Write at least three sentences using words from the story. Make sure your sentences show what the words mean.

Words from the Story

crank	summon	disorderly conduct	pale	fastened
seething	countless	irate	spare	bellowing

_____

_____

_____

_____

_____

_____

_____

Directions: Answer this question.

1. Why are the animals **seething** and **irate** at the end of the story?

_____

_____

Analyzing the Literature

Provided below are discussion questions you can use in small groups, with the whole class, or for written assignments. Each question is written at two levels so you can choose the right question for each group of students. For each question, a few key points are provided for your reference as you discuss the book with students.

Story Element	Level 1	Level 2	Key Discussion Points
Character	How does the dragon feel when he sees Elmer?	What is the dragon's reaction to Elmer rescuing him?	The dragon is excited. He encourages Elmer to hurry and calls to say where he is located. Also, once cut free, the dragon runs in circles and tries to turn a somersault.
Plot	What new problem does Elmer have when he finds the Dragon Ferry sign?	Describe the dilemma Elmer has when he locates the Dragon Ferry sign.	Elmer is unsure how to get the dragon's attention without being too loud. He needs to find a way to cross the river to tell the dragon he is there.
Setting	Why can't Elmer walk through the river?	How does the author let you know that Elmer doesn't want to walk through the river?	Elmer thinks the river is too muddy to walk through. He would not be able to make it to the other side. He is also scared about what unknown things might be in the river.
Plot	How does Elmer use the lollipops he packed?	Explain the importance of the lollipops Elmer packed in his knapsack.	Elmer uses the lollipops to create a bridge out of the crocodiles so he can cross the river. Then, the moody first crocodile starts swimming down the river. The other crocodiles want to finish their lollipops so they follow. This causes the "crocodile bridge" to carry all the other animals away down the river.

Name _____ Date _____

Reader Response

Think

Think about a time when you solved a difficult problem. How did you figure out your solution?

Informative/Explanatory Writing Prompt

Describe the steps you take to solve difficult problems. What do you do to think of solutions and then choose the best one?

_____

_____

_____

_____

_____

_____

_____

_____

_____

_____

Name _____ Date _____

Guided Close Reading

Look at the picture at the end of chapter 10. Then closely reread the last two pages of the book.

Directions: Think about these questions. In the chart, write ideas or draw pictures as you think. Be ready to share your answers.

❶ Use details from the picture to describe what has happened to all the animals on Wild Island.

❷ Based on the events in the story, how do you think Elmer feels now that he has achieved his dream of flying?

❸ Use what you know about Elmer's mother to predict what might happen to Elmer and the dragon if they return to Elmer's home.

Name _____ Date _____

Making Connections—Rhyming Words

Directions: When you write a song or poem, you can choose to have some words rhyme. Usually, the rhyming words are at the ends of the lines. Write a song or poem describing the area where the dragon is held. Have at least three sets of rhyming words in your song or poem.

Name _____ Date _____

Language Learning-Spicy Synonyms

Synonyms are words that have the same meaning. Good writers use synonyms to help add excitement to their writing. Ruth Stiles Gannett uses the synonyms of *raging*, *seething*, *furious*, *irate*, and *ranting* to describe the animals when they realize the dragon is escaping.

Directions: Create a thesaurus on your own paper. A thesaurus is a book where you can find synonyms for words. Use at least four words from the story. Some words are suggested below.

Each page in your thesaurus should have the following items on it:

- the original word at the top
- a sentence using one of the synonyms
- a list of at least two synonyms
- a picture illustrating the original word

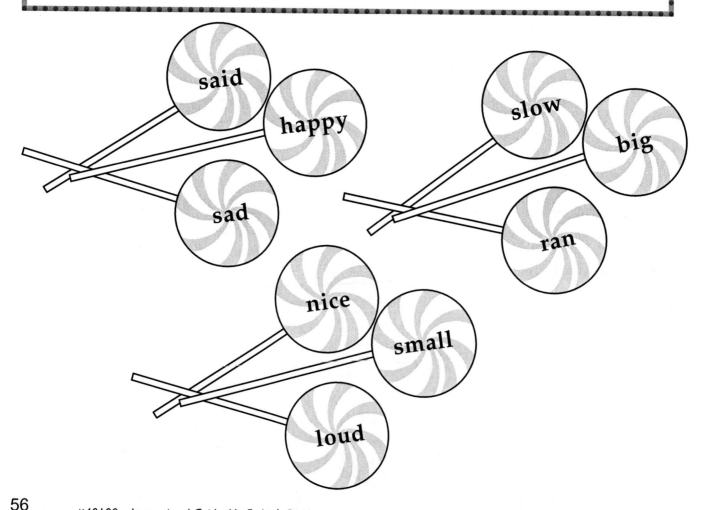

Name _____ Date _____

Story Elements-Character

Directions: Write a letter to Gorilla to try to persuade him to free the dragon. Your letter should list reasons why it is unfair to keep the dragon and why it may be helpful to Gorilla that the dragon be let go.

Dear Gorilla,

_____

_____

_____

_____

_____

_____

_____

_____

_____

_____

_____

_____

Name _____ Date _____

Story Elements-Plot

Directions: What if Elmer had not had lollipops in his knapsack to use to trick the crocodiles into helping him cross the river? Think of a new way that Elmer could have crossed the river, and draw a picture of his new solution. Write a title for your picture.

Name _____ Date _____

Post-Reading Theme Thoughts

Directions: Choose a main character from *My Father's Dragon*. Pretend you are that character. Draw a picture of a happy face or a sad face to show how the character would feel about each statement. Then describe how the character feels.

Character I Chose: _____

Statement	How Does the Character Feel? ☺ ☹	Why Does the Character Feel This Way?
Helping others is very important.		
Getting others to do your work is fair.		
If you are scared, then you are not being brave.		
It is better to solve problems with your brain than with violence.		

Name _____ Date _____

Culminating Activity: My Own Dragon

Directions: Work with students to help them choose one of the following activities. Most likely, these activities will require adult assistance to complete. The masks on pages 61–63 may be fun for students to use as they perform these different activities. Also included, on page 63, are body outlines for Elmer and the dragon in case students want to use these in their activities.

- Write a story similar to *My Father's Dragon*. This time, though, pretend you are saving an animal of your choice from the zoo. What problems might you face along the way and how would you solve the problems in a way like Elmer? Try to have your story closely mirror the book. Publish your story in a book and include illustrations.

- Create a three-dimensional model of Wild Island and the characters. You may use supplies like construction paper, leaves, sticks, clay, popsicle sticks, or anything else you find helpful to display the setting and characters of the story. Then, use this model as a stage to recreate the story showing how Elmer tricked the animals to eventually rescue the dragon.

- Write a reader's theater script retelling the events of the book in order. Then, use the masks or stick puppets from pages 61–63 for Elmer and the dragon. You can also make masks for the various animals in the story. The masks should be decorated to show the markings and colorings of each of the animals. Once your script is complete, perform your reader's theater with a group of friends.

Culminating Activity: My Own Dragon (cont.)

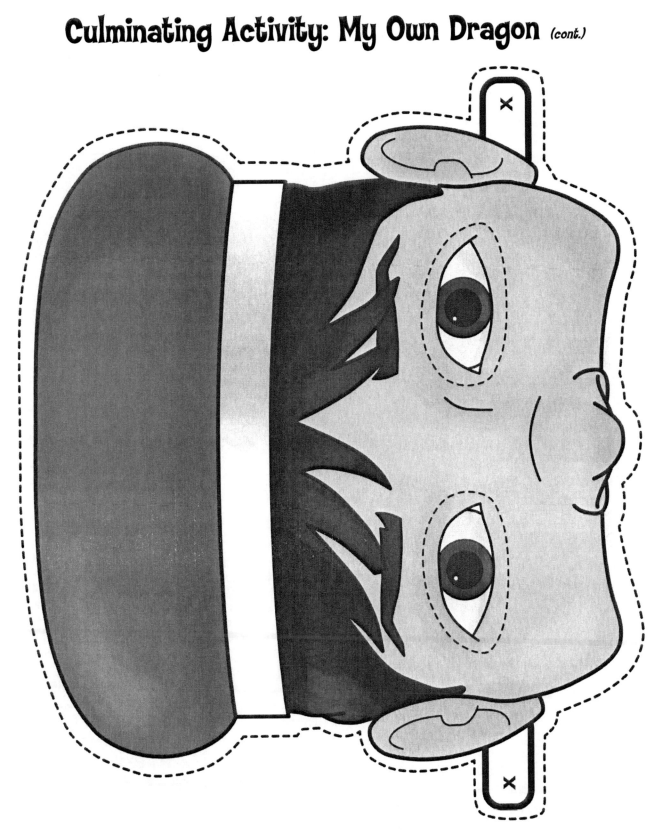

Elmer

Culminating Activity: My Own Dragon *(cont.)*

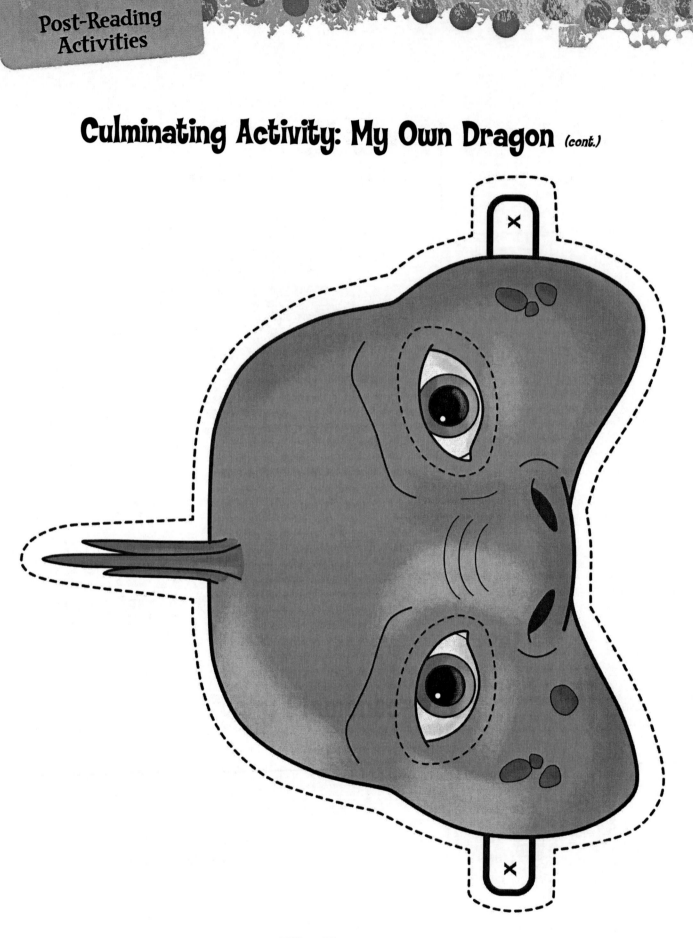

The Dragon

Culminating Activity: My Own Dragon (cont.)

Name _____ Date _____

Comprehension Assessment

Directions: Fill in the bubble for the best response to each question.

Chapters 1–2

1. Which quotation from the book shows how the animals are lazy?

(A) "This was going to end all their crossing-the-river troubles."

(B) ". . . they used to hate having to go all the way around the beginning of this river to get to the other side of the island."

(C) "His only friends are the crocodiles . . . ."

(D) "Why, this is just exactly what we've needed all these years!"

Chapters 3–4

2. Why does Elmer not give up when his journey to the island is so hard?

(E) He wants to travel and see the island.

(F) He doesn't want to go back home.

(G) Cat told him he had to see the dragon.

(H) It is important to Elmer to rescue the dragon.

Chapters 5–6

3. What shows how the animals are unhappy that Elmer is on their island?

(A) The animals keep trying to catch Elmer and hurt him.

(B) The dragon is forced to fly the animals across the river.

(C) Boar is very bossy to the other animals.

(D) Mouse keeps messing up his words.

Comprehension Assessment (cont.)

Chapters 7–8

4. Describe how Elmer is helpful to both Lion and Gorilla.

_____

_____

_____

_____

_____

_____

_____

Chapters 9–10

5. What shows that Elmer and the dragon dislike the island?

   Ⓐ "... as the dragon soared above the dark jungle ...."

   Ⓑ "... we'll start on the long journey home."

   Ⓒ "... nothing in the world would ever make them go back to Wild Island."

   Ⓓ "As my father and the dragon passed over the Ocean Rocks ...."

Name _____ Date _____

Response to Literature: Character Matters

Directions: Even though the animals keep trying to hurt Elmer, he never hurts them back. Elmer is a kind hero because he rescues the dragon without hurting any of the animals along the way. Pick your favorite way Elmer shows kindness to one of the animals. Draw a picture of that scene in a neat and colorful way. Then, use that same scene to answer the questions on the next page.

Name _____ Date _____

Response to Literature: Character Matters (cont.)

1. How is Elmer showing kindness in this scene?

_____

_____

_____

_____

2. Why is this your favorite scene?

_____

_____

_____

_____

3. Why is it important to always show kindness?

_____

_____

_____

_____

Name _____ Date _____

Response to Literature Rubric

Directions: Use this rubric to evaluate student responses.

Great Job	Good Work	Keep Trying
☐ You answered all three questions completely. You included many details.	☐ You answered all three questions.	☐ You did not answer all three questions.
☐ Your handwriting is very neat. There are no spelling errors.	☐ Your handwriting can be neater. There are some spelling errors.	☐ Your handwriting is not very neat. There are many spelling errors.
☐ Your picture is neat and fully colored.	☐ Your picture is neat and some of it is colored.	☐ Your picture is not very neat and/or fully colored.
☐ Creativity is clear in both the picture and the writing.	☐ Creativity is clear in either the picture or the writing.	☐ There is not much creativity in either the picture or the writing.

Teacher Comments: _____

_____

_____

_____

Name _____ **Date** _____

_____

_____

_____

_____

_____

_____

_____

_____

Name _____ Date _____

_____

_____

_____

_____

_____

_____

_____

_____

_____

_____

_____

_____

_____

_____

The responses provided here are just examples of what students may answer. Many accurate responses are possible for the questions throughout this unit.

Vocabulary Activity—Section 1:
Chapters 1–2 (page 15)

1. The animals **inhabited** Wild Island.

Guided Close Reading—Section 1:
Chapters 1–2 (page 18)

1. Students need to reference the list of items and write a relevant prediction.
2. Elmer packs household items rather than weapons. He is brave for thinking that ribbons, toothpaste, and other everyday items will keep him safe from wild animals.
3. Students should compare their own ideas with the list of items actually packed.

Making Connections—Section 1:
Chapters 1–2 (page 19)

1. 1 + 1 + 7 = 9 items
- Students should compose word problems using data provided on the page. Students should also employ proper sentence structure, correct punctuation, and appropriate word choice when writing a solvable word problem.

Language Learning—Section 1:
Chapters 1–2 (page 20)

- Students should use the illustration and the details from chapter 2 to describe the physical and character traits of the dragon using adjectives.

Vocabulary—Section 2:
Chapters 3–4 (page 24)

- Elmer goes on an adventure because of the **extraordinary** cat.
- As Elmer gets closer to Wild Island, the **rumbling** noise of the snoring whale gets louder.
- He is never late to an important meeting, so the merchant is a **punctual** man.
- The mouse is considered to be **unreliable,** so the animals do not believe him.
- **Solemn** and nervous, the animals discuss the possibility of an intruder on the island.
1. The **invasion** that the animals are discussing is actually Elmer coming to the island.

Guided Close Reading—Section 2:
Chapters 3–4 (page 27)

1. Elmer is overheard sneezing and has to pretend to be Monkey. He almost walks between two boars.
2. "...if there had been an invasion, *I* would have seen it."
3. He really wants to save the dragon from being hurt, and Elmer wants to fly.

Making Connections—Section 2:
Chapters 3–4 (page 28)

Goods	Services
wheat	loading a ship
tangerines	baking bread
fishing	delivering bags
cranberries	growing corn

Story Elements—Section 2:
Chapters 3–4 (page 30)

- **Wild Island**—Only animals live there. It has a dragon. There are no tangerine trees. The river almost cuts it in half
- **Similarities:** Both are islands, have trees, and have rocks. Elmer visits both
- **Island of Tangerina**—Humans live on it. It has ports and lots of tangerine trees.

Vocabulary Activity—Section 3:
Chapters 5–6 (page 33)

- Elmer walks along the **bank** of the river.
- The jungle is too **dense** to walk through easily.
- Elmer is surrounded by seven tigers while in a **clearing**.
- The tigers are chewing gum, so the animals know there is an invasion **afoot**.
- Elmer **wades** in a small pool of water, not knowing what is in it.
- The **dim** jungle prevents Rhinoceros from seeing his tusk.

Guided Close Reading—Section 3:
Chapters 5–6 (page 36)

1. Elmer most likely feels tired and unsure if this is a good idea, and he wonders what might happen next.

2. Phrases from the book include: gloomy and dense, sticky leaves, tripping over roots, couldn't squeeze between trees, hard to walk through. Students may pull more phrases from the pages that describe a difficult setting for walking.

3. Elmer keeps going and doesn't give up. He isn't scared off by the animals.

Making Connections—Section 3:
Chapters 5–6 (page 37)

- **Carnivores:** Students should draw and label any meat food items.
- **Omnivores:** Students should draw and label both meat and plant food items.
- **Herbivores:** Students should draw and label any plant food items.

Language Learning—Section 3:
Chapters 5–6 (page 38)

- The words in alphabetical order and spelled correctly are: beautiful, chewing, dragon, hungry, jungle, monkey, mud, private, tigers, trespassing.

Story Elements—Section 3:
Chapters 5–6 (page 39)

1. The hungry tigers are excited to eat a little boy. **Elmer offers the tigers some gum.**
2. Elmer wades into what he thinks is an empty pool of water. **Elmer gives Rhinoceros some toothpaste to help clean his dirty tusk.**

Vocabulary Activity—Section 4:
Chapters 7–8 (page 42)

1. Lion thinks his snarled, messy mane is **dreadful**.
2. Elmer quietly watches the **dignified** lioness walk by.
3. The monkeys think the magnifying glasses are **miraculous**.
4. The monkeys **frantically** try to get all the fleas off Gorilla.
5. Lion keeps his mane **tidy** to please his mother and to get his allowance.

Guided Close Reading—Section 4:
Chapters 7–8 (page 45)

1. He should go to the right toward the "Dragon Ferry."
2. Lion's mother is so dignified that she walks with her nose in the air and doesn't notice Elmer.

3. Students should write an adventure that relates to the other signs labeled as "Beginning of the River" or "Ocean Rocks."

Story Elements—Section 4:
Chapters 7–8 (page 48)

- Lion threatens to eat Elmer.
- **Elmer shows Lion how he can braid his mane to keep it tidy.**
- Elmer comes across Gorilla.
- **Elmer offers Gorilla a magnifying glass to see the fleas more clearly.**
- The rest of the monkeys come down to see the new object Elmer gives out.
- **Gorilla and the monkeys are too busy picking off fleas to notice Elmer's escape.**

Vocabulary Activity—Section 5:
Chapters 9–10 (page 51)

1. The animals are **seething** and **irate** to see the dragon escape the island, because now they can no longer be lazy.

Guided Close Reading—Section 5:
Chapters 9–10 (page 54)

1. The animals are all on the backs of the crocodiles and riding down the river.
2. Elmer most likely feels thrilled, excited, and proud for finally realizing his dream of flying.
3. Students should describe how Elmer's mother may react when he brings home a dragon. Student responses may vary, but they should make sense with what we know about the characters.

Comprehension Assessment
(pages 64–65)

1. B. "... they used to hate having to go all the way around the beginning of this river to get to the other side of the island."
2. H. It is important to Elmer to rescue the dragon.
3. A. The animals keep trying to catch Elmer and hurt him.
4. Elmer helps Lion by showing him how to clean his mane, which is important because Lion's mother is coming to visit. Elmer helps Gorilla by giving the monkeys magnifying glasses, which will help them see the bugs that make Gorilla itch so much.
5. C. "... nothing in the world would ever make them go back to Wild Island."